50
Little Tips
That Make A
BIG
Difference

By: Nancy J. Friedman
The Telephone Doctor

30 Hollenberg Court
St. Louis, MO 63044
314-291-1012
www.telephonedoctor.com

CREDITS
Editor: Valerie Phillips
Publisher: Independent Publishing Corporation

Copyright 2005
By Nancy Friedman, The Telephone Doctor

Printed in the United States of America
   by Independent Publishing Corporation

This book is dedicated to:

All who make a difference.

LITTLE TIP #1

Don't chew gum or have anything in
your mouth
(other than your tongue)
when you're talking with a customer.

"A gum chewing girl and
a cud chewing cow.
They both look alike, but there's a
difference somehow.
Ah yes, I have it now.
It's the thoughtful look
on the face of the cow."

Source: An Ann Landers column

LITTLE TIP #2

Don't kid yourself.
Yes – they CAN hear that smile.

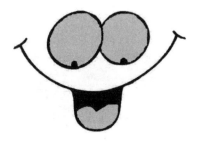

Remember:
A phony smile is better than a real frown.

A frown is a smile…upside down.

Keep that smile in your voice and on your face.

It DOES matter!

LITTLE TIP #3

When sending a package to someone,
especially a customer, enclose a note.

A little note keeps it from being impersonal.

And don't forget to date it.

> Telephone Doctor
>
> *6-1*
>
> *Hi Bob –*
>
> *Here's the article we talked about.*
>
> *Look forward to talking to you soon.*
>
> *Nancy*

LITTLE TIP #4

Don't use military jargon on civilians.

Abbreviations can be dangerous.
KWIM?
(Know what I mean?)

LITTLE TIP #5

Best to ASK if you can put a caller on
the speakerphone.

Placing a caller on a speakerphone
<u>without asking</u> is inconsiderate.

LITTLE TIP #6

And speaking of speakerphones,
never answer or terminate a phone call
on a speakerphone.

It's best to pick up the receiver
and say hello or good-bye.

LITTLE TIP #7

Always ASK a caller if
they are able to hold.

Putting someone on hold without asking
(You've had it happen – "Hold on."
Click) remains a big frustration of the
American public.

LITTLE TIP #8

Call waiting should NOT be on a
business line.

It can cause interruptions at very inopportune times and can easily offend the other party causing them to feel unimportant.

Have call waiting for the teenagers, not your customers.

LITTLE TIP #9

One-word answers can be perceived
as cold and rude.

Nope

Uh-huh

No

Yes

Use full sentences.
Three words make a sentence.

"Yes" and "No" are not complete
sentences. It sounds as though you're in a
hurry to get rid of the person.

LITTLE TIP #10

Screening telephone calls at its best is
intimidating.
At its worst – humiliating.

Why screen calls at all?

LITTLE TIP #11

Always return phone calls…or have them
returned on your behalf.

There's no excuse not to return a phone call **or** have it returned on your behalf.

LITTLE TIP #12

Respond to most NON-spam emails
unless the message received clearly
closes the exchange.

A few words will suffice.
It assures the message was received.

How much more simple could answering
an email be than hitting a few keys?

(Even if to tell the sender "please don't
email me anymore.")

LITTLE TIP #13

<u>Never</u> hang up on <u>anyone</u>.

Exceptions:
Obscene and computer calls.

When we hang up on someone,
we label ourselves as rude.

LITTLE TIP #14

Never tell a customer to "call back."

It's our job to call the customer back
(if a callback is necessary at all).

The best practice is to handle the
situation on the first call if at all possible.

LITTLE TIP #15

Give your full attention to the person
you're speaking with – on the phone or
in person.

You cannot do two things well at once.
Make eye contact if you're face-to-face
and "ear contact" on the phone.

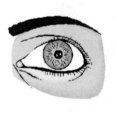 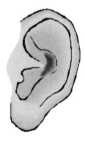

LITTLE TIP #16

Never take up two parking spaces.

Well, that's what my dad told me.

(Piggy, Piggy)

LITTLE TIP #17

Put the toilet seat back DOWN.

Just do it!

It's the nice thing to do.

LITTLE TIP #18

Take your kids out of a public area when they're screaming – but never silence their laughter.

Gently remove the little ones to an area
where you can calm them down.

On the other hand – let them laugh. The
sound of youngsters laughing is golden.

LITTLE TIP #19

Use your turn signal to go
from lane to lane.

The other drivers aren't mind readers.

It's like not returning a phone call –
just rude!

LITTLE TIP #20

Send flowers to your mother
on **<u>YOUR</u>** birthday.

You'll be glad you did.
It's a special day for her too!

LITTLE TIP #21

There's no need to raise your voice
when talking on a cell phone.

Yet so many do.
Wonder why?

LITTLE TIP #22

Never use swear words when you need
help from anyone.

You want their help,
not their animosity.

Learn to swear
BY people –
not AT them.

LITTLE TIP #23

Deliver products and services when you
say you will (or before).

That's the old
under-promise
and
over-deliver
thing.

LITTLE TIP #24

Learn to negotiate.

It's better to lose a battle
and win the war.

LITTLE TIP #25

Never rifle through your spouse's
personal things.

That's what my mom told me.

(Get someone else to do it –
Just Kidding!)

LITTLE TIP #26

Don't whisper in someone's ear when others are near you.

They'll feel you're talking about them
(and you probably are).

LITTLE TIP #27

Never roll your eyes at a customer,
co-worker or family member behind their
back.

They do have eyes
in the back of their head!!!

LITTLE TIP #28

Take good care of your eyes,
teeth and feet.

It's worth the money.

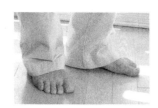

LITTLE TIP #29

Pay full and rapt attention to the flight attendant's speech (every time).

Better to know and not need than need
and not know.

LITTLE TIP #30

When servicing a customer –
really service the customer.

Give 100% attention.

Hold your conversation with another employee until the customer is out the door or off the phone.

Give

100%

LITTLE TIP #31

Your Mom was right!
Please, thank you and you're welcome
are "magic words."

Does this tip even need an explanation?

LITTLE TIP #32

Take (or make) your cell phone calls
away from other people.

Cell phones are great, but we don't need, or want, to be a part of someone else's conversation.

LITTLE TIP #33

Cover your mouth when you yawn
(or cough or sneeze)!!

Yee gads! I can't believe the number of people that don't. YUK!
Germ showers!

LITTLE TIP #34

Have food in your mouth?
Don't chew with an open mouth.

Keep your mouth closed!
There is no "seefood" diet.

LITTLE TIP #35

When you step on someone's toes or accidentally bump into someone – say "excuse me."

It lessens the frustration and
it's the right thing to do.

LITTLE TIP #36

When making a phone call, ask your party if they have "time to talk" before rushing into what you need.

Without this permission, you are indeed barging in and are an interruption.

LITTLE TIP #37

It's USELESS to argue with a customer.

You will NEVER win the argument.

LITTLE TIP #38

Learn how to change a negative
into a positive.

Negative beginnings are often ineffective. Start with a positive.

LITTLE TIP #39

Make your own phone calls.

Having someone else ask for your party
is often regarded as self-imposed
important.

LITTLE TIP #40

Don't ask someone else to lie for you.
("Tell them I'm in a meeting." – when
you're not.)

You may as well get on the phone
yourself and say,
"Hi, I'm not here right now."

Having someone lie for you
marks you as dishonest.

LITTLE TIP #41

When leaving your phone number on voice mail, leave it twice…and slowly.

314-291-1012
314-291-1012

Rushing through the phone number
makes the person rewind several times.

P.S. – Break up the last 4 digits
for even more clarity.

314-291-10 (ten) - 12 (twelve)
314-291-10 (ten) - 12 (twelve)

LITTLE TIP #42

Never have your home answering
machine say, "We're not home right
now" or "There's no one here to answer
your call."

All you need to say on a home answering machine is either your name or a phone number. Both are not necessary. Then ask the calling party to leave you a message.

"... Please leave a message."

LITTLE TIP #43

Put a nice little handwritten note on any
letter you send out to a customer.

Just a "HI" or "THANKS" after your signature makes it more personal. One of those little things that will make a big difference.

~ ~ ~

~ ~ ~
~ ~ ~

~ ~ ~ ~ ~ ~ ~ ~ ~ ~
~ ~ ~ .

~ ~ ~

Talk with you soon.
N.

LITTLE TIP #44

Keep your voice mail greeting updated.

Outdated greetings can cause
problems for your callers.

LITTLE TIP #45

To get people to return phone calls, try
leaving a stated 'deadline.'

Stated deadlines work better than, "Call me ASAP." Try, "Bob, I need to talk with you before noon on Friday the 7th."

LITTLE TIP #46

Make 'no ulterior motive' calls to customers. It will brighten their day.

A "NUM" call.

A NUM (no ulterior motive) call is that short call to a customer that says, "Hi, I was thinking of you and wanted to say HI."

No sales pitch necessary…just a plain old NUM call.

Works wonders!

LITTLE TIP #47

When taking a message for someone, it's better to say, "I'll see that they get the message" rather than, "I'll see that they call you."

We are not responsible for that person making the call.

Delivery is our job – not execution.

LITTLE TIP #48

When speaking face-to-face with someone, make good eye contact.

If you're looking around, you'll appear
aloof and unconcerned.

LITTLE TIP #49

Wake up in a good mood.

It'll last the whole day long.

LITTLE TIP #50

Don't be "too busy to be nice."

Nice does matter. And when you're too busy to be nice, you're bound to hurt feelings.

OOPS!

I lied.

There are more tips.

LITTLE TIP #51

On your voice mail greeting, tell your callers where you ARE, not where you aren't.
"Hi, I'm not here right now."
DUH!

Use the short amount of time on that greeting for something that is of value.

LITTLE TIP #52

Be on time for meetings.

Latecomers disturb the session
inconveniencing others
who were on time.

LITTLE TIP #53

If you take the last of ANYTHING,
let someone know
(or replace it yourself).

How frustrating it is to go for an item and there isn't one. Who took the last of something without telling?

In fact, when you're getting low – let someone know!

LITTLE TIP #54

Show appreciation – constantly.

Even for things you take for granted.

LITTLE TIP #55

Your kitchen and bathroom are public rooms.

Keep these two rooms in good order
and your house or office
will always appear neat.

(Remember: These are 'public rooms.')

LITTLE TIP #56

Learn all six touch points of
communication.

We interact with all of them:

- 🖳 Email
- 🖷 Fax
- ❩ Voice Mail
- ✉ US Mail
- ☎ Phone
- ☺ Face-to-Face

LITTLE TIP #57

Don't take office supplies
for personal use.

Call it what you want –
it's still stealing!

LITTLE TIP #58

Never OK a negative.

Example:

Customer: "I'm having trouble with the computer I bought."

You: "OK."

It is NOT OK.

Instead try,
"I'm sorry that's happening."

LITTLE TIP #59

Management must speak the same
language as employees.

It sets a good example.

LITTLE TIP #60

When taking messages – refrain from
saying, "He's all tied up."

Here is a picture of what the caller perceives.

LITTLE TIP #61

When placing someone on hold…tell the truth on estimating how long you think it will take to get what they need.

"Hang on a second" is a big old FIB.
Start telling the truth.

(Liar Liar Pants on Fire…
Nose as Long as a Telephone Wire.)

LITTLE TIP #62

Always have a PLAN B.

Having an alternative plan when working with customers is an important part of helping them.

Plan A??
Plan B??

LITTLE TIP #63

Be prepared for the unexpected.

Learn to roll with the punches. Things don't always go the way we want them to. Expect the unexpected.

(It's why you have a Plan B.)

LITTLE TIP #64

Avoid self-imposed pressure.

(Known as SIP.)

It's like making a mountain
out of a molehill.

LITTLE TIP #65

Avoid excuses.

Excuses only tell someone,
"I'm not going to help you now."

LITTLE TIP #66

Learn to laugh at yourself.

The most fun you can have is making fun of yourself before someone else does.

THE END

(of the book – not the tips)

There are thousands of them.
We'll be back!

Thank you!

Nancy

About the Author
Nancy Friedman, The Telephone Doctor

Nancy founded her company, Telephone Doctor, in 1983. She was named 'The Telephone Doctor' by an editor of the Quad City Times in Davenport, IA.

She was born and raised in Chicago, IL. Nancy and her family now reside in their headquarter city of St. Louis, MO. Her son, David, is vice president & general manager of Telephone Doctor and her daughter, Linda Steinberg, is client service manager of their other business, Weatherline, Inc.

Nancy's theatrical background has brought her a thriving career in public speaking. She was selected as one of St. Louis' top 25 business women and has appeared on national TV and radio along with being published in the *Wall*

Street Journal and many other magazines and newspapers around the country.

Telephone Doctor is an international customer service training company with training videos available in 28 countries and 7 languages. Nancy also delivers an energetic, motivational program for associations and corporations around the country.

Additional services offered are small group workshops delivered by a trained certified Telephone Doctor facilitator.

Other books by Nancy are: Customer Service Nightmares, Telephone Skills from A to Z, Telemarketing Tips from A to Z and How to Develop Your Own Customer Service Training Program.

To reach Nancy, email her at
nancy@telephonedoctor.com.